Another Year Single

AHNI HANCOCK

Another Year Single

TRUSTING GOD'S PLAN WHEN YOU FEEL

LET DOWN AND LEFT OUT

Another Year Single

Copyright © 2024 Ahni Hancock

All rights reserved. No part of this book may be reproduced or transmitted in any form or by any means without written permission from the author.

ISBN: 9798324774646

DEDICATION

This book is a tribute to the rare ones—the single women whose love for the Lord remains steadfast through every season and circumstance.

CONTENTS

Foreword   10

Introduction: Rare   16

Part 1: Identity

     1. He Prepares A Place   30

     2. Turn The Lights On   36

     3. Conversation With God: #1   51

Part 2: Lament

     4. He Sits In The Dark With Us   60

     5. Conversation With God: #2   71

     6. Reminders For The Hard Days   78

Part 3: Surrender

     7. Trust   84

     8. Conversation With God #3   94

Part 4: Whole

     9. Walking In Surrender   102

Epilogue

     The Recipe   120

     Fireworks   122

     From Matt   130

Group Discussion Starters   134

Beyond The Pages   144

Acknowledgments 170

About The Author 172

Foreword

<u>Viviane Castillo-Manzano</u>

I've known Ahni since she was Anita, my younger sister's friend and music video companion in elementary school. She would shut herself in the piano room for hours at a time if allowed to do so and play the day away. I watched her transition to high school as a shy teenager trying not to make waves, a bit of a loner, it seemed, but always with this spark of "I'm different." Instead of the traditional pale pink quinceañera dress to celebrate her 15th birthday, Anita's dress was red. As a college student, Anita knew her passions rested in art and music, and she took a while to figure out how they fit into the rest of her life. I was at her art shows and music album release events, watching her share her gifts with others. There was always a good turnout for Anita. She had a really strong group of friends. Once, we joined her (and them) for tacos, and all the tables joined together didn't fit all the friends! She wasn't loud at all, but she always stood out with a different vibe, complete with a leather jacket and high heels on her already 5'10" frame, and that attracted people to her. When she made the shift to a career that she swore she would never take on, she thrived. As an art teacher, Ahni had an impact on students beyond creating art, which she did well. She provided a space in which each child was valued. Within an environment of chaos and noise, Ahni's classroom brought peace, recognized by her students and peers as "good vibes."

In each of these stages, the one constant was that Ahni had a burning desire to honor God. Whether it was through art, music, or other ministries, I watched as she honed in on a calling to bless young girls. As her calling became more refined, so did her outreach. Her burden for uplifting young women to realize the potential they had been created with led her to the creation of Crowns, a ministry designed to invest in the self-worth and strength that came from knowing that your Creator designed you perfectly and that His plans were perfect. I was floored when she invited me to join a Crown conference. She had put together a team of women who were utilizing their individual strengths to create an environment where women of all ages were loved, and their lives poured into with powerful testimonies, worship that brought you to the feet of Jesus, and where beauty and excellence came through the details as a demonstration of how valuable each guest was to Crowns. As her influence increased, so did the pressure to maintain a high standard. People took notice, and Ahni was a role model, beginning with my own daughter, who looked up to Ahni as the coolest person ever! I am so grateful that Kamila had such a cool older friend who made loving Jesus such a normal part of doing life…because no area of Ahni's life was outside the reach of His influence. No area of her life was exempt from being called to holiness, even if it was different than what was the norm around her.

I remember a conversation over coffee when she said, "I know what I want. I want a husband who is passionate about Jesus, and I won't…I can't settle." The challenge of living that conviction, not just preaching it, came as Ahni saw friends and peers moving in and out of relationships, sometimes resulting in great joy, many times settling because "what if this is the best there is." Her desire was not singleness, but the pool of options to change that situation was virtually non-existent because her standards were high. She was too picky, some said. The years continued to pass by, and Ahni found contentment, "I want to be married, but if this is what God wants for me, He is enough." We discussed the qualities she valued that she wasn't willing to give up, and we talked about wish list items, too. Through it all, Ahni's conviction was that singleness would produce in her what her Lord deemed necessary to prepare her for His will.

When Anita met Matt, she was ready. She had learned the source of her worth, trusted through the storm, and found that the God she had entrusted all the years of her life to was a good God, with or without the answer she was praying for. In His perfect will, God prepared Anita to take a leap of faith in order to enjoy His goodness toward her through Matt. It gives me such joy to see her living the life she had dreamt of for so long. She learned that the Giver of dreams is also the Fulfiller of those dreams, in His perfect time. I encourage you to read her story as if you were having coffee or tacos with Anita today. Glean from her testimony the courage to trust God, and love Him fiercely through your own season of singleness, even when it hurts, and especially when your life story is different than all the stories around you.

"Tell my daughters I love them."

Introduction

Rare

"EXISTING ONLY IN SMALL NUMBERS AND THEREFORE VALUABLE OR INTERESTING."

My face flushed with embarrassment as I sat on the exam table at the doctor's office. I kept my gaze low to avoid eye contact with the doctor. I thought he would be on my side, praising me for choosing abstinence. Still, instead, I sat there listening to his words - words that belittled me for being 31, single, and a virgin. I had gone to see the doctor because this unwelcome feeling, known as anxiety, was becoming too familiar.

    He asked me if I was sexually active. My response was that I had never been sexually active and that I was waiting for marriage. His expression shifted from concerned to surprised. "But you are a 31-year-old woman," he said. "You should be sexually active with a man or woman." He set his clipboard down, shook his head, and continued, "You are not living a *normal* life. I know this sounds taboo, but you should have graduated college, had a job, married, and had kids at your age. But you don't have anyone. You are alone." I wish you could hear the frustration in His voice. His reaction surprised me a bit.

"But I don't feel lonely. I have great relationships with my friends and fam-"

"Your friends and family have someone to go home to. They have a boyfriend or spouse. But you? You have no one."

Is this really happening to me?! Can he say this to me?

"Here is what you need to do," he continued, "you need to go to a bar, have a drink, and meet some guys. You need intimacy."

Hot tears blurred my vision as I marched out of the doctor's office in anger and disbelief at what had just happened. His words played like a loop in my head.

You don't have anyone to go home to.
You are alone.
You should be married.
You should have kids.
You are not living a normal life.

The doctor was right when he said my life did not look like other women my age. I was 31, single, and saving myself for my husband. I had never been in a bar, never experienced intimacy, not even a kiss. (Hold up, girl, it's not that I didn't want to!) Of course, I wanted to feel a man's lips on mine, get married, and experience all the things that God created for marriage, but at 31 years old, there was no sign of that coming soon, not even a preview.

No *(take a breath)*, I was not *normal*.
I was *strange*.
I was *rare*.

> **RARE:**
> - EXISTING ONLY IN SMALL NUMBERS AND THEREFORE VALUABLE OR INTERESTING
> - UNUSUALLY GOOD OR REMARKABLE

If you've picked up this book, chances are you may have had a similar experience. Perhaps, like me, you find yourself feeling *rare* in your circle, not living a "normal" life. There may have been moments you felt belittled because you chose abstinence, or along the way, you opened the door to secret sin that ushered in shame. While you maintain your trust in God while waiting for a husband, you can't escape the feeling that some pain still lingers. Those nights when you lie in bed and realize you've lived *another year single*, another birthday single, another holiday single…can make the loneliness real. You have carried questions like, "*God, why does the younger girl get a guy first when I have been serving you longer than she has been saved?! God, what else do I need to learn so I can move on to my next season, marriage?! God, why are you hurting me this way?!*"

Friend, I hear you, and God does too. I wrote this book with you in mind because I remember being in your shoes and needing to hear that it's okay if my life looked different than other women my age. This book isn't another round of pep talks about how great single life can be. By now, you've likely heard it all. It's not a manual on finding the right guy or mastering the dating game. You've probably exhausted those sermons and self-help books that may sound like, '*God has a perfect plan for you!*' or '*Just keep trusting in Him a little longer.*' While those points are

Rare CHECK LIST

- [ ] YOU ARE LIVING AGAINST POPULAR CULTURE AND CONTINUE TO SAY YES TO HOLINESS.

- [ ] MODESTY IS STILL IMPORTANT TO YOU.

- [ ] YOU ARE SINGLE AT AN AGE IN WHICH MOST WOMEN ARE MARRIED AND HAVE CHILDREN.

- [ ] YOU ARE A VIRGIN OR ARE NOW PRACTICING ABSTINENCE BECAUSE WAITING TILL MARRIAGE IS STILL SOMETHING YOU VALUE.

- [ ] YOU UNDERSTAND THAT PURITY IS NOT JUST ABSTAINING FROM SEX BUT ALSO ABSTAINING FROM WHAT YOU SEE AND WHAT YOU LISTEN TO.

- [ ] YOU HAVE NOT BEEN CHOSEN, AND YOU STILL SERVE.

- [ ] YOU MIGHT HAVE FELT LET DOWN AND LEFT OUT, BUT YOU CONTINUE TO PUT YOUR TRUST IN THE LORD.

valid, many are quiet about the dark and grieving moments we walk through in our singleness. Wanting to be a wife and a mother is a normal desire for a woman. In our society, these desires are recognized and embraced as integral parts of a fulfilling life. So when you are not following the "normal" life like my doctor said that I wasn't, you feel some ache stirring in you that can leave you feeling let down and left out.

  When Matt entered my life at 34, he became more than just my husband—he was my first kiss, my only boyfriend, and the man I waited for and gave my all to. Abstinence, modesty, and surrender are often seen as old-fashioned values. In today's society, where sexuality is often twisted and excused by calling it "progressive", it's crucial to remember that God has not changed his mind about purity. He is still calling us to holiness. The world has told us to give in to our self-desire when the Word says to die to self. (Holiness isn't just about abstaining from specific actions. It's also choosing holiness in what we watch, listen to, and say. We must be intentional about what we allow into our lives.) Rare, can sometimes seem like you're a bit of an odd duck. But it's those unique qualities that make you a hidden treasure. In today's society, the rarity of a single woman maintaining abstinence is often belittled. Yet, this rarity is like a breath of fresh air in a world full of conformity. It is a countercultural stance, one that aligns with Christian principles.

> **COUNTERCULTURE**
> - A GROUP OF PEOPLE WHO DO AND BELIEVE THINGS OUTSIDE OF WHAT SOCIETY CONSIDERS NORMAL OR TYPICAL

Christian single women, you are supposed to be countercultural! You are not supposed to blend. We have swallowed the lie that our lives have to look like everybody else's, dress like everybody else, pose for pictures like everybody else, etc. The truth is that we do not have the same posture as the culture. The people around us *should* recognize that there is something different about us - something *rare*. It's comfortable to blend, but that is not biblical.

> *"Do not conform to the pattern of this world,*
> *but be transformed by the renewing of your mind."*
> Romans 12:2

I will not shy away from standing for purity, and I invite you to join me in raising a standard for Christ. Even when it seems like we're going against cultural norms, let us not diminish this light of Jesus within us. The generations that follow us need to witness women committed to living according to *His* truth.

I sat with my parents in their living room two days after that doctor's appointment. The weight of the doctor's words still lingered in my head. *You don't have anyone to go home to. You are alone. You are not living a normal life.* As I sat with my parents, I was ready to talk about it. I refused to conform to the culture of the world. I wanted to live *rare* and tell someone of the disturbance I wanted to cause on the enemy's plan.

"Anita, what did the doctor tell you?" my mom asked. I shared every detail of the doctor's words with my parents. After silence settled for a moment, I saw my dad looking back at me. With a calm yet firm voice, he said, *"That man does not know God's calling over your life. He does not know God's plans for you."*

Just like my father's voice spoke over me, God speaks over you today. Feelings of worthlessness, of being left out or left behind, do not have a say in what God is actively doing in your life. However belittled you have felt by society, family, church, coworkers, maybe even a doctor, they do not know God's calling over your life. They do not know the plans God has for you.

Friend, I can't explain why you find yourself single. I wish I knew why wonderful, God-fearing women remain unmarried. What I can offer you is my own experience as a testimony that God is good and He is faithful. I'll share parts of my story - a journey through the 'whys,' the pain, and the surrender that led me to discover wholeness in Jesus. Still, most importantly, I want to guide you to honest conversations with God that fearlessly embrace the sad, dark, and grieving moments we walk through. I hope this book presses you to uncover a deeper dialogue with God about a prayer you began praying 10, 15, maybe 20 years ago. A simple yet meaningful prayer that may have sounded like, *"Hey God…where is my husband?"*

The norms of this world may say that a fulfilling life for a woman is one with marriage and kids. Still, I dare to say there is a *rare* kind of wholeness in Christ Jesus for the single woman who continues to put her trust in the Lord even though she has felt let down and left out. The journey to being complete and whole in Christ is not dependent on what your outside looks like. While the world offers a path to wholeness through self-sufficiency, it's a journey reliant on human strength alone. But the wholeness found in Jesus is carried by *His* unfailing strength. It's surrender—a letting go—that unlocks this profound sense of completeness. Through the pages of this book, I want to guide you to this beautiful surrender.

Friend, this is my invitation to you: join me in unraveling this honest dialogue with God, surrendering all to Him, and embracing this rare kind of living. The vision is to see women who are completely in love with and devoted to their Creator, where the longing for His presence is above all other desires. This rare kind of living may look revolutionary to a world that leans towards selfish pursuits. Another year single, another holiday single, another birthday single, and even so, blessed are you for raising a standard of purity, faith, and trust for the Lord. Friend, *you* are the hero in this book - uniquely created, set apart, and hidden to shine for such a time as this.

You are rare.
You are uncommon.
You are exceptional.
You are remarkable.
You are wonderful.
You are stunning.
And you are whole in Jesus' name.

Takeaway Points:

- Embrace your rarity and the fact that you're living a life that goes against the culture.
- Your commitment to purity and faithfulness makes you a rare gem in a world that often values conformity.
- Despite societal pressures and expectations, hold onto your convictions and continue to prioritize your relationship with God above all else.

How to Read the Book:

Throughout the book, you'll find some journaling prompts labeled "Draw Near." These prompts are like gentle nudges, encouraging you to dive a little deeper into the heart of each chapter.

Now, when you come across the section called "Conversations with God," it's time to create your own sacred space. Find a quiet corner and carve out some unrushed moments. Think of it as your special date with God, where you can be without any hurry or distractions.

While it's awesome to share this book with friends and chat about it together (there are group discussions for each part at the back!), "Conversations with God" are your personal moments. Take your time, be open, and embrace the beauty of vulnerability. It's your chance to connect with God in a way that's uniquely yours. Enjoy every moment!

Part 1: Identity

He Prepares A Place

"What do you notice?" my counselor gently asked, inviting me to dive into my past during our weekly therapy sessions. With her guidance, I began remembering memories and noticing what God was revealing. My mind flashed back to a moment of my childhood I had forgotten, an experience that I had buried beneath layers of confusion and shame since I was eight years old. As a 36-year-old woman, I hesitated to share with my counselor. With doubt and fear, I thought, "What will she think of me?" Panic wanted to keep me shut, but a gentle whisper of the Holy Spirit said, *"It's time to heal."*

    I would later understand that my brain was hiding painful memories, and as life went on, I built a life on a fractured foundation. If I refused to deal with the pain that day, I knew that at some point, I would crumble.

I imagined my brain as a house with memories categorized and stored in different rooms. I felt the Holy Spirit lead me to a back room. In a dark corner, I noticed a pile of painful childhood memories like dirty laundry. From the bottom of the pile, I pulled out this shameful moment. *"Ok, God. This is a long overdue conversation, huh? It's now or never."* With a lump in my throat, I managed to begin telling my counselor the memory I noticed God reminded me of. I was about eight years old, playing at a neighbor's house. The friend I played with was older than me, and I was a follower.

Now that I'm older, I can see that my friend must have been sexually abused. It was being demonstrated in the way my friend played with me. "I knew it was wrong," I said to my counselor. "I should have said no and walked away, but…I couldn't move." For 28 years, my brain hid this unwanted, shameful memory. And there, with the guidance of my counselor and the Holy Spirit, I was finally getting rid of it.

The whole process felt like she led me to the entrance of a dark valley. Lighting up a pathway with a lamp of wisdom, she led the way and brought me to a safe house. At the door of this house, Jesus was waiting for me. He welcomed me into His embrace, offering comfort for my pain. As I sat by the warmth of the fire he had prepared for us, He wrapped me in a blanket and sat beside me. Enveloped in His love, we talked…and we talked…and we talked, sharing intimate conversations of what caused my heartache. He wiped my tears, cupped my face in His hands, and whispered words of reassurance, *"I was there. I have always been there."*

I understood that I was in an unknown and uncomfortable situation at such a vulnerable age. The burden of guilt and shame was lifted, and I left my therapy session overwhelmed by the realization that Jesus had been waiting for me all along, creating a sacred space for us to talk.

The Plan

I am deeply grateful for the presence of God, who invites us to sit and talk with Him. His voice settles the rumbling in our hearts and minds, bringing order to the chaos that surrounds us. With a stirring, a gentle nudge, He calls us to draw near and sit with him. As I began planning this book, I asked God what He wanted to do through it. This theme of intimate conversations kept pressing in my heart - a longing to reconnect with you, His daughter. I imagine you've had moments where you've poured out your heart to God, asking him to help you understand why things are the way they are. At times, you may have felt ignored, questioning how a God who promises to speak and answer prayers could seem silent. Friend, I've walked through similar seasons. In my journey as a single woman in my early thirties, my relationship with the Lord changed because of the honest and intimate conversations we had.

Friend, the message in this book is nothing new. There are no new trendy ideas for the Christian single woman. No quick-fix solutions. Because truthfully, the message has always been the same - it's Jesus. He is the focus of every season in our lives. If I stray from making Him the center, I have completely ruined the purpose of this book.

I have created exercises and guided conversations in the coming pages to draw you closer to our Heavenly Father.

These moments of dialogue are intended to deepen your relationship with Him as you navigate singleness, discovering a rare kind of wholeness reserved for you, the single woman. Now, I can't promise you will find the answers to your "why" questions within these pages. But I can assure you that every moment spent in the presence of God is never wasted. So, may you answer the stirring of the Holy Spirit as you begin this journey. And may you feel the gentle touch of your heavenly Father cupping your face as He whispers those precious words, *"I'm here. Come and meet with me."*

Reconnect with My Daughters

As I sat down to begin writing this book, I asked the Lord for guidance. I asked God what He desired to accomplish through these pages, and this is what I felt Him say…

> *"My daughters have been hurting in the waiting.*
> *My plan has sometimes been painful for them.*
> *They may have believed that I was holding out on them.*
> *I want to reconnect with my daughters.*
> *I want them to take my hand again.*
> *My plan has always been designed to know them. Not to forget them.*
> *My waiting has caused them pain.*
> *It has made a dent in their hearts and trust in me.*
> *Tell my daughters I love them.*
> *Tell them I never meant to cause them pain.*
> *The unknown is a scary place. I know. I see it all.*

*I know they have felt as if I wasn't speaking; I have been.
I know it's been painful when they have cried out asking for answers; I heard them.
I know they have felt I was absent; I have always been here.
I could have given them what they asked for, but they would have been miserable.
With a snap of my fingers, I could have removed their pain, but they would have never gained what choosing me through the pain can do.
Tell my daughters I love them."*

Takeaway Points:

- Jesus patiently waits for us in our darkest moments, ready to embrace us with love and comfort.

- Intimate conversations with God are essential for deepening our relationship with Him and finding peace amidst life's chaos.

- While answers to our "why" questions may not always come, every moment spent in God's presence is valuable and never wasted.

Turn The Lights On

"MY SCARS ARE FILLED WITH THE GLORY OF GOD."

Let me take you back to 1999, a time when every girl in my 8th-grade Biology class was head over heels for NSYNC. Before our teacher started class, the tables students shared were covered with posters and CDs of the boy band heartthrobs. Pages of Teen Bop magazine flipped frantically, all while the boys in our class rolled their eyes. Meanwhile, my shy and quiet self was still listening to cassette tapes on my dad's Walkman. Girls my age were into Justin Timberlake, and I was into Spanish worship artist Marcos Witt. I wasn't interested in the latest trends. I never quite fit in, and it felt unnatural to try. Deep down, I sensed a calling to live differently.

You see, I was raised in a Christian household. My father was an assistant pastor at a small church in deep south Texas, and my mother, a homemaker, stood beside him, nurturing his calling.

Together, an example of a beautiful partnership, with God at the center. I'm sure I recited the sinner's prayer at every Sunday school or VBS class at church. But at eight years old, something changed. One summer night, my dad came into the bedroom I shared with my sisters before going to sleep. With a chair in one hand and a bible in the other, he sat with us and told us a bible story. That night, he shared with us about Jesus and His sacrifice for us. I'm sure I heard the story of Jesus on the cross many times before, but that night, it was as if I was hearing it for the first time - His word is *alive*. My dad led me to Christ that night. I can still see this picture of myself lying face up on the top bunk I shared with my older sister and feeling aware of being separated from the world. This desire to live in a way that honored God was planted in me. And even though I was just a kid, I was determined to let Him use my life for His purpose.

    As a child, I wrote songs to God, sang specials on Sundays at church, and danced in my bedroom to praise and worship. One particular Saturday afternoon stands out to me. I was about ten years old, and as I was raking leaves and listening to "*Motivo de mi Canción*" by Marcos Witt - I felt God's presence while doing chores. I knew *Him*, and He knew me.

    What the world offered was not attractive to me, so the enemy went after my identity. Like most teen girls, I went through low self-esteem and self-image issues, feeling ugly and unwanted. I knew I was called to live differently, but the human part of me still wanted to be liked and accepted by others.

    I developed an eating disorder in 9th grade. While researching anorexia and bulimia for a class presentation, I stumbled upon websites that were going to affect the rest of my life. Back then, school computers lacked the internet protection measures we have today. I clicked on a website that taught girls how to become anorexic and bulimic. Dark imagery of skeletons and thin bodies filled every space on the website, giving girls tips on how to hide their eating disorders from their families, body positions to ease the hunger pains, and easy ways to purge food. I started imitating what I saw on that website, believing that a skinny body would make me feel pretty and normal. This cycle continued for the next five years.

At 19, I was a student at Christ for the Nations Institute in Dallas, TX. One night, my roommate and I talked about how we wanted to get skinny, so we cut out magazine images of models in bikinis and taped them all over our kitchen. We hoped that seeing these pictures would prevent us from eating. The following day, we left for class, and when we returned that afternoon, we noticed that someone had been in our apartment. There were pieces of paper taped over every magazine image with bible verses declaring God's love for his children and the beauty of his creation. I stood in our apartment kitchen speechless and with remorse. I had decided to corrupt the body God made me responsible for, and even after failing, He still wanted me.

"God…how can I not choose you?" I whispered back to Him. I took down the images, threw them away, and I was done with it. That day, I gave this area of weakness to the Lord.

I returned home to South Texas and graduated from a local university. I was very much involved in ministry, but even so the enemy continued to go after my identity. I got a job as a high school art teacher. I was teased by coworkers and called "virgin ears" for being unfamiliar with sexual words and phrases that were thrown around in conversation. One evening, I began to search online for the meaning of the words I was unfamiliar with.

One-click led to another until I opened a dark door that took years to shut. 60.2% of women have seen pornography, and I became part of that statistic.

His Kindness Leads Us to Repentance

    For years, I struggled to answer an altar call at church. The fear of being exposed and possibly embarrassed held me back. But it wasn't just about bringing my sin to light but also about how others might treat me. I was in leadership, and there wasn't much talk about a plan to guide people back to healing; it felt more like being cast out. My greatest fear was the thought of confessing my sin to people who might not understand how to handle it. My church did not feel like a safe place for me, so I kept what I had done silently.

    I continued in ministry but couldn't fully function in my gifting due to the shame and secret burden lingering in my mind. Sometime after, I went on a worship ministry trip with my friends. We led worship, and after the service, the church leaders gathered around our team to pray for us. One of the leaders began praying for me, and as I bowed my head and listened, in a quiet, loving tone, he said to me, "The Lord has shown me an area of pain and disappointment he has brought you out of. He is saying, 'I am going to use it for my good.'" I was in tears as I realized that my biggest fear—being shamed when exposing my sin—didn't come true. Instead of shouting so that everyone could hear, the leader spoke softly into my ear. In that moment, the shame I had carried for so long was transformed by God's love. When it was brought to light of God, what had felt shameful and isolating became a moment of profound love and acceptance. I knew that I was truly loved, faults and all.

*Don't you see how wonderfully kind, tolerant,
and patient God is with you? Does this mean nothing to you?
Can't you see that his <u>kindness</u> is intended to <u>turn</u> you
from your sin?*
Romans 2:4 (NLT)

Sometime after, I opened up to a friend about this, someone who would continue to love me and pray with me even after knowing my shame. And I am so thankful that she continues to be one of my best friends. Through the work of the Holy Spirit and a Christian counselor, I learned to surrender daily and come out of that pit.

You might wonder if I should have kept this to myself. But let me be clear—I'm not keeping this hidden. I'm bringing it to light for the sake of other young women reading this who may be dealing with similar struggles, feeling like they have no one to turn to in their community. I refuse to let shame silence me when speaking out could set someone else free. Today is not the day to hide.

The truth is, as a single woman waiting for a husband, you do not get to pause your sex drive. You are not excluded from sexual jokes at work, school, or even among unsaved friends. Before you dismiss yourself from this conversation, consider the media you consume—the shows you watch and the music you listen to. Those scenes on your TV or phone may seem harmless, but they can impact your heart and mind. Watching mature-rated content on Netflix might feel like a sign of maturity. Still, your spirit may be saying something else entirely. A small dose of gratification can lead down a dangerous path.

If you have struggled with sexual sin, know that you're not alone. I love you, and more importantly, the Lord loves you, too. I've prayed for you, asking God to meet every woman who reads this book and has wrestled with these issues. May He guide you toward transformative steps in your journey, starting right now.

His Power is Made Perfect in Weakness

Christian living does not ensure a covering of having a weakness, a struggle, or even falling into sin. The apostle Paul had a personal struggle that he called a "thorn in the flesh," which hindered his ministry. Just like the apostle Paul, we all have our own 'thorns in the flesh.' But here is the beautiful truth - we have God's grace in those moments of weakness. His power works best and is complete in our weakness.

> *"but He has said to me, "My grace is sufficient for you [My lovingkindness and My mercy are more than enough—always available—regardless of the situation]; for [My] power is being perfected [and is completed and shows itself most effectively] in[your] weakness." Therefore, I will all the more gladly boast in my weaknesses, so that the power of Christ [may completely enfold me and] may dwell in me."*
> 2 Corinthians 12:9 (AMP)

When you feel like you're not strong enough to resist temptation or overcome sin alone, God's power is most evident and available. So, instead of dwelling on your weaknesses, focus on His strength.

A while back, I met up with a young sister in Christ over coffee. As we sipped our drinks, she bravely shared with me about wrestling with a hidden struggle. She had opened the door to pornography. The look of relief on her face when I told her, "Girl, I've been there too. I understand," was priceless. We both shed tears, and my heart ached to think she had been carrying this burden alone. It broke me to know she wasn't sure if she could trust anyone with her story at first. But I was glad that my honesty strengthened her. She needed to know that stumbling doesn't define you and that God's grace can lift you up no matter what. Walking away from that conversation, I couldn't shake the feeling that there were more young women out there silently battling the same shame. Just like Paul, through our struggles, we can grow in character, humility, and ability to empathize with others. It's why I can openly share this part of my story, recognizing God's grace at work. His power triumphs over our weaknesses.

You can either keep your weaknesses hidden or bring them out into the light before the Lord. It's okay to ask for help. Reach out to a trusted leader or friend, or consider counseling if you need extra support. Find the root that opened the door to sin.

This is your sister in Christ, calling out to you to come out of that. I want you to stand with me and make war against the evil one. Younger sisters are coming after us and need to see women boldly living for the Lord. What the world considers 'normal' differs from what God's kingdom sees as normal. In

God's kingdom, it is *not* normal to sin. Do not allow sexual scenes or perverse language not to bother you anymore. Let's never lose our spiritual sensibility. There's a 'normal' of this world and a 'normal' of the kingdom of God. Which one are you choosing to live in?

Stones of Help

I found myself sharing with my counselor a vivid image that had formed in my mind—it was a timeline of my life. Tears filled my eyes as I noticed something. Over every painful memory, I could see the hand of God over every year, every month, every day. He stood over each moment, never hiding from me.

I also saw large stones fall from heaven, stomping on the ground, landing over these difficult seasons of my life like timestamps. Each stone seemed to declare, 'Here, at this moment in time, God intervened.'

In Samuel 7:12, we learn how Samuel set up a stone and named it Ebenezer to commemorate God's help after a victory over the Philistines. This stone served as a memorial - a reminder of God's unwavering faithfulness and His constant presence in times of trouble and need.

Just as Samuel set up a stone to commemorate God's presence in that battle, our own painful experiences can serve as markers of God's presence and intervention. We can look back unafraid and without shame, recognizing those moments when God guided us through darkness into restoration. Our weaknesses become Ebenezers in our lives—testimonies of God's love and grace, reminding us of His faithful intervention.

It is possible to feel worthy.
It is possible to feel lovely.
It is possible to be whole.

"God," I whispered, remembering my stones, "what do you want to say to your daughters through this?"

"Tell them my hand has always been upon them.
I want to restore layers of unresolved memories.
Moments they couldn't walk away from.
Their seasons of pain, I'm turning them into stones of remembrance.
They will not be afraid or ashamed to look back.
They will see that I have always been with them.
I am their father.
I love them.
Tell them to come, sit with me."

MY HUSBAND MATT KEEPS A SMALL ROCK ON HIS SIDE OF THE BATHROOM SINK. I FIRST NOTICED IT AFTER WE GOT MARRIED AND I MOVED IN. I'VE CLEANED THE BATHROOM COUNTER MANY TIMES, AND HE'LL REMIND ME NOT TO THROW AWAY THE SMALL ROCK. WHEN WE MOVED INTO A NEW HOME A YEAR AND A HALF LATER, THE ROCK CAME WITH US AND STILL SITS ON HIS SIDE OF THE SINK TODAY. THE STONE IS MEANINGFUL TO HIM - IT'S HIS EBENEZER STONE. HE PICKED UP THE STONE THE DAY HE WAS ABANDONED AND HIS PREVIOUS MARRIAGE CAME TO AN END. THE STONE SERVES AS A REMINDER OF GOD'S PROMISING REDEMPTION.

Takeaway Points:

- God's kindness towards us leads us to repentance; He will never shame us.
- God's power is most evident and available in our moments of weakness, allowing us to grow in character and humility as we rely on His strength.

- Ebenezer stones serve as tangible reminders of God's promises and redemption in our lives, symbolizing His faithfulness and presence in both joyful and challenging seasons.

Draw Near

Turn the Lights on

Before you dive into your first conversation with God, I want to offer you a chance to come out of hiding. Perhaps you will skip this because you genuinely have not struggled with sexual sin. But I cannot move forward without creating a space in this book to talk about this. So, if this does not resonate with you, feel free to move on to the next part. But if it does, I want you to know I'm proud of you.

Are there any cracks in your foundation? Are there any dark corners in your house that need to be brought into the light? Maybe you will write it in this journal or write it on a separate sheet of paper.

No more hiding.
No more secrets between us.
Turn the lights on.
Let me come in.

Let's shed light on those hidden corners. In the following lines, I want to encourage you to open up to God and share with Him the struggles you've faced. Reflect on the emotions you experience when you think about this shameful part of your life. Write down any guilt, shame, fear, or regret that comes to mind. Consider how hiding this part of your life has affected your relationship with God. Have you felt distant from Him? Be honest and transparent, knowing He already knows your heart but desires you to come to Him with your burdens.

End with thanksgiving - thanking Him for what He will do with your story.

(Check out an extra journal prompt in "Beyond the Pages" on the page 146 titled "Next Steps.")

Conversations with God: Identity

Prepare:

What an incredible journey you are about to embark on! These parts of the book, "Conversations with God," are meant to be quiet and intimate moments in His presence. One of the most challenging things people have when talking with God is making time to be silent. This is going to take intentionality. You may need to set dates with God, where you will put your phone on silent mode during this time, or leave it in another room to avoid picking it up and scrolling. Sometimes, background music without words helps quiet the noise in the mind. I encourage you to silence your mind so it may be filled with God's presence.

I find it helpful to set up an empty chair either next to or in front of me to represent God's presence in the room. If you feel comfortable, I encourage you to do that in every conversation you have with God throughout this book.

The first conversation with God aims to help you lean in and listen to His voice while also affirming your identity. Remember, a conversation is a two-way exchange. I'll invite you to ask God a question and listen to what He says. As you read, allow your God-given imagination to guide you, pausing after each sentence to absorb the words. There is no wrong answer here, so release any fear or pressure of getting it right. You are simply responding to the gentle nudge, the whisper of the Holy Spirit saying, "Come and meet with me." So, envision yourself sitting with your Heavenly Father, engaging in a beautiful conversation. Let's start!!

Conversation #1

Picture God standing before you, smiling at you.
He opens his arms wide open and invites you into His arms.
Lean in and feel His strong arms wrapped around you and the safety of who He is.
Rest your head against His chest and listen to His heartbeat for you.
Stay in his arms for a moment, feeling the warm embrace of your Father.
This is what being loved and held feels like.
There, in the comfort of his arms, ask Him this question,
"God, what do you love about me?"

Take a moment to close your eyes and let Him speak to you...

Write down the words He shared with you below.

_____
_____
_____
_____
_____
_____
_____
_____
_____

This is the Father speaking identity over you. He has been waiting to meet with you in that place.

It feels so good to be loved, huh :)

Part 2: Lament

Through it all I have learned this profound truth – it's possible to have great joy and weep at the same time.

He Sits In The Dark With Us

"IT IS DOUBTFUL WHETHER GOD CAN BLESS A MAN GREATLY UNTIL HE HAS HURT HIM DEEPLY."
AW TOZER

Since I was a little girl, I've felt a strong calling to music ministry. In 2019, close to the end of an album production, I experienced the devastating loss of all my music files. Sure, I was angry at the person who chose to get rid of my music, but I was more hurt that God allowed it to happen. *God, did I hear you wrong all this time? Were you not calling me to music?* I began questioning whether I had misunderstood God's calling to music ministry and doubted I could hear His voice. I felt like a fool, as if I had been played.

I sat alone in my living room for hours until daylight faded and darkness filled the room - hurt, angry, and bitter. But something happened in my living room. As the outside lights filtered through my living room window, I noticed the empty chair a few feet away from where I sat. At that moment, I felt the presence of God sitting in the dark with me. I didn't see God with my eyes, but I knew he was there. I didn't hear Him speak, but His presence said more than a thousand words. His nearness held me. And even after I complained and told Him how angry I was, He stayed with me.

Months passed, and still, I carried questions about the future - why my plans seemed to stall. I sat with the Lord again to talk and realized a deep layer of pain stemming from my singleness. Not having answers about marriage or a sign of a husband hurt. The questions often surfaced when I was alone, like driving in the car or lying awake at night. *What is wrong with me? Why not me?*

Suddenly, the words spilled out of my mouth: "God, you hurt me." It was honest, and I felt comfortable enough to say that, yet a part of me was taken aback at the audacity of such a statement. If God does not hurt His kids, why did His plan cause me so much pain? Why didn't he intervene or speak to me when I needed a word from him? He knew I felt forgotten and left out, the stink of being made fun of. With every emotion laid before God, my Father, I questioned my boldness, hoping I wasn't overstepping a line. And you know what happened next? My honesty attracted His healing power as I felt the roots of pain being gently removed. This nearness with God created a deeper intimacy with Him. He sat in the dark with me over and over again. He never left me.

Countless books exist that strengthen you during the wait for your husband. There are journals and devotionals that guide you on how to make the most out of your season of singleness, revealing all the beautiful things you can do while you're single. While those books are necessary, it is also needed to talk about the pain. Sadness. Moments of withdrawal and even grief. For a long time, I ignored the hurt that came with being single. I didn't want God to think that I was ungrateful, and I surely didn't want to be led by emotions, but I didn't know how to release them.

I caught myself repeating lines and prayers that sounded cliche. I mean, God knew what I truly meant, right? These memorized lines were shallow and not a genuine communication with God. I found comfort in knowing that the bible is full of people with emotions similar to mine and yours. They, too, cried out to God and asked him why. There is something so beautiful and comforting about the fact that at the center of the bible is the book of Psalms, where writers share honest feelings with God. Songs and prayers that express deep sorrow, pain, and distress.

"How long, O Lord? Will you forget me forever? How long will you hide your face from me?"
- Psalm 13:1

"My tears have been my food day and night…"
- Psalm 42:2

"Give ear to my prayer, O God, and hide not yourself from my plea for mercy! Attend to me, and answer me; I am restless in my complaint, and I moan."
- Psalm 55:1-2

"O Lord, God of my salvation; I cry out day and night before you. Let my prayer come before you; incline your ear to my cry! For my soul is full of troubles, and my life draws near to Sheol."
- Psalm 88:3

"Will the Lord reject forever? Will he never show his favor again? Has his unfailing love vanished forever? Has his promise failed for all time? Has God forgotten to be merciful? Has he in anger withheld his compassion?"
- Psalm 77:7-9

LAMENT = A PASSIONATE EXPRESSION OF GRIEF OR SORROW

Friend, we *can* walk through moments of lament. You want to know how - we lament *with* God. To lament is not to lose your faith or be ungrateful. It is the safety of crying *with* God and knowing the emotions do not lead you but you can be *in* them. It is saying to God, "I acknowledge who you are, and I also acknowledge my pain." These emotions humanize us and can lead us to rediscover who we are and who God is. We are God's creation, God made, dependent on Him, and He…oh, friend, He is creator, sovereign, mighty, and our Father.

> **IT'S NOT JUST ABOUT WHAT YOU ARE CRYING ABOUT.**
> **IT'S WHO YOU ARE CRYING WITH.**

These psalms reflect the human experience of suffering, grief, and the raw emotions individuals bring before God in times of distress. Here is an incredible thing about the psalmists. They often move from lament to expressions of trust and hope in God. They don't stay in the pain and hopelessness.

"But I trust in your unfailing love; my heart rejoices in your salvation. I will sing the Lord's praise, for he has been good to me."
- Psalm 13:5-6

"Why, my soul, are you downcast? Why so disturbed within me? Put your hope in God, for I will yet praise him, my Savior and my God."
- Psalm 42:11

"I love the Lord, for he heard my voice; he heard my cry for mercy. Because he turned his ear to me, I will call on him as long as I live."
- Psalm 116:1-2

"I wait for the Lord, my whole being waits, and in his word, I put my hope."
- Psalm 130:5 (NIV):

He is Growing Something Beautiful

After losing my music, I struggled to write songs again for months. My journaling was dark, without inspiration. But I kept returning to the piano. I knew that even if my words made no sense, God would still be pleased that I kept trying. As I sang and tried to play with words one night, the Lord gave me this line…

*"God, you are growing something beautiful
in the dark places."*

These words were a promise I held on to, trusting God would grow something meaningful out of my dark and painful seasons. The line also reminded me of this imagery from Isaiah 55:13, a beautiful promise in which God transforms hardships into flourishing.

*"Where once there were thorns, cypress trees will grow.
Where nettles grew, myrtles will sprout up.
These events will bring great honor to the Lord's name;*

they will be an everlasting sign of his power and love."
Isaiah 55:13 (NIV):

This verse offers us hope and reassurance that God has the power to transform areas of hardship into something beautiful and fruitful. We can trust in His ability to bring redemption out of something that may have caused pain. This transformation is not just for our benefit but also serves to glorify and showcase God's power. He can turn our trials into testimonies, bringing great honor to His name.

Here is an insight that I am experiencing today in my own life: the suffering you go through isn't just for you. Your suffering is also for the person watching you. Others are coming behind you who will need your life as an example, drawing strength and encouragement from the way you navigate your struggles. The crushing is so that you comfort others with the comfort you have been given.

Pain to Purpose

Picture this: in John 9, Jesus and his disciples encounter a man who is blind from birth. In their curiosity, the disciples ask about the cause of his blindness, asking if it was due to his sin or that of his parents. It's a question that resonates deeply with our own struggles, isn't it? We often wonder if our pain, loneliness, or secret battles result from something we've done wrong.

1 As he went along, he saw a man blind from birth.

> *2 His disciples asked him, "Rabbi, who sinned, this man or his parents, that he was born blind?"*

A common belief in Jewish culture was that suffering was the consequence of sin. In verse 3, Jesus corrects this assumption with a profound and unexpected statement.

> *3 "Neither this man nor his parents sinned," said Jesus, "but this happened so that the works of God might be displayed in him.*

Jesus redirects their focus away from assigning blame to recognizing an opportunity for God's glory to be revealed through the man's suffering. Friend, your struggle is not a punishment for something you've done wrong. Your loneliness, your battles - they are not meaningless. Just as Jesus saw beyond the blind man's affliction as an opportunity for God's glory to shine forth, He sees beyond your pain to the greater purpose He has in store for you. Your struggles are not a reflection of your worth or your faith. Instead, they are an opportunity for God to display His power, grace, and love in your life. Whether emotional, mental, or physical, God redeems tragedies and transforms them for *His* glory - that is the ultimate goal.

Draw Near

Reflect on the idea that our suffering can serve as a testimony to others. Have you ever found comfort or encouragement in someone else's story of overcoming hardship? How might your own experiences of pain and growth inspire and encourage others?

Takeaway Points:

- Despite feelings of hurt and anger, we can experience the tangible presence of God in our darkest moments. He sits in the dark with us.
- We can embrace vulnerability and honesty in our relationship with God without fear of judgment. He longs to hear our joys and sorrows.
- Lamenting with God allows for authentic emotional expression without losing faith.
- The Psalms demonstrate a pattern of moving from lament to expressions of trust and hope in God, inspiring us to hold onto hope amidst our own struggles.
- Lamenting with God is not a sign of weakness but of profound strength. It leads to a deeper understanding of ourselves and God's character, reaffirming His role as creator, sovereign, and loving Father.

Conversations with God: Lament

Prepare:

Do you need to lament with God? Perhaps you find yourself mourning the years you believe you've lost, longing for the role of wife or motherhood. It's okay to grieve those dreams with the Lord. Maybe you need to be honest with the pain you experienced through the waiting.

Take time in a quiet place and get raw and honest with God about your pain. God is the only one who can walk with us through those dark valleys and bring us safely to the other side. Don't miss the opportunity to say, "This is what I've truly been carrying." The goal is to be honest with God, release the load, and gain intimacy with the Father.

Prepare by reading Psalm 23

> *"The Lord is my shepherd; I have all that I need.*
> *He lets me rest in green meadows; he leads me beside peaceful streams.*
> *He renews my strength.*
> *He guides me along right paths, bringing honor to his name.*
> *Even when I walk through the darkest valley, I will not be afraid,*
> *for you are close beside me.*
> *Your rod and your staff protect and comfort me.*
> *You prepare a feast for me in the presence of my enemies.*

You honor me by anointing my head with oil.
My cup overflows with blessings.
Surely your goodness and unfailing love will pursue me all the days of my life,
and I will live in the house of the Lord forever."

"You honor me by anointing my head with oil."

Anointing with oil was a common practice in ancient Israel as a symbol of blessing, honor, and hospitality. In Psalm 23, we see God as the host, and it was customary for hosts to anoint the heads of their guests with fragrant oil. Imagine entering God's presence as if walking into His home, greeted by a beautifully set table with a feast prepared just for you. Picture yourself being anointed, enveloped in the fragrance of His presence.

Conversation #2

Before: Find a quiet spot. Pray and ask God to silence your mind. Remember to pause after each sentence.

> *Picture God waiting for you, standing outside the door of His home.*
> *He raises His hand to wave at you, and His smile is breathtaking.*
> *As you approach, His arms open wide and take you in.*
> *With his arm around you, you both enter His home, knowing He anticipated your coming.*
> *Inside, you find the table has already been set.*

White linen, flickering candles, vibrant flowers, and a spread of your favorite dishes - a feast prepared with loving care by the best host imaginable.
Amidst the table's beauty, you notice something else: pictures of trials, struggles, pain, and hardships you've gone through and are currently on the journey.
God says, "I've prepared a meal for you, but first, I will anoint your head with oil."
As he pours the fragrant oil over you, you feel a sense of protection and strength for what is to come.
It gets dark in the house.
The candles offer some light, but the brightest light is the radiant presence of God.
He sits beside you in the darkness.
With gentle compassion, He invites you, "My daughter, tell me your lament… I'm listening."

In the lines below, tell God your lament.

_____
_____
_____
_____
_____
_____
_____
_____

As you conclude your prayer of lament, just like the psalms, end with an expression of hope by writing down a bold prayer of hope and trust in God.

_____

_____

_____

_____

_____

_____

_____

_____

_____

_____

_____

_____

_____

_____

_____

_____

_____

_____

_____

_____

_____

_____
_____
_____
_____
_____
_____
_____
_____
_____
_____
_____
_____

    Oil was also used to consecrate or set apart individuals such as kings, priests, and prophets for a sacred purpose. The act of anointing symbolized God's chosen ones being set apart for His service and empowerment. I pray for this anointing oil over your life. And that as you've finished releasing this prayer of lament with God, you may come out enveloped, smelling like the aroma of His presence, knowing you are set apart for a purpose.

    Lord, embrace your daughters. Hold them. Comfort them. Fill their hearts with your desires.

Reminders for the Hard Days

When we are in the middle of the pain, how easily we forget the promises of God. It's in those moments when we need voices of hope speaking into our lives. As a sister, let me be a voice in your ear, lifting you up and reminding you of the God you serve and how much He loves you. Affirm your faith with these verses…

- *"The Lord is close to the brokenhearted and saves those who are crushed in spirit."* Psalm 34:18

- *"And we know that in all things God works for the good of those who love him, who have been called according to his purpose."* Romans 8:28

- *"For I know the plans I have for you, declares the Lord, plans for welfare and not for evil, to give you a future and a hope."* Jeremiah 29:11

- *"But blessed is the one who trusts in the Lord, whose confidence is in him. They will be like a tree planted by the water that sends out its roots by the stream. It does not fear when heat comes; its leaves are always green. It has no worries in a year of drought and never fails to bear fruit."* Jeremiah 17:7-8

- *"But those who hope in the Lord will renew their strength."* Isaiah 40:31

- "Though the mountains be shaken and the hills be removed, yet my unfailing love for you will not be shaken nor my covenant of peace be removed," says the Lord, who has compassion on you." Isaiah 54:10

- "Come to me, all you who are weary and burdened, and I will give you rest. Take my yoke upon you and learn from me, for I am gentle and humble in heart, and you will find rest for your souls." Matthew 11:28-29

- "And my God will meet all your needs according to the riches of his glory in Christ Jesus." Philippians 4:19

- "Take delight in the Lord, and he will give you the desires of your heart." Psalm 37:4

- "For my thoughts are not your thoughts, neither are your ways my ways," declares the Lord." Isaiah 55:8

- "Now to him who is able to do immeasurably more than all we ask or imagine, according to his power that is at work within us." Ephesians 3:20

More of what pain produces...

Pain is not desirable, but it refines us. The verses below tell us more of what pain produces.

Wisdom:
- Psalm 119:71 (NIV): "It was good for me to be afflicted so that I might learn your decrees."

Greater Compassion for Others:
- 2 Corinthians 1:3-4 (NIV): "Praise be to the God and Father of our Lord Jesus Christ, the Father of compassion and the God of all comfort, who comforts us in all our troubles, so that we can comfort those in any trouble with the comfort we ourselves receive from God."

A Deeper Relationship with God:
- Philippians 3:10 (NIV): "I want to know Christ—yes, to know the power of his resurrection and participation in his sufferings, becoming like him in his death."

Perseverance:
- Romans 5:3-4 (NIV): "Not only so, but we also glory in our sufferings, because we know that suffering produces perseverance; perseverance, character; and character, hope."

Character Development:
- James 1:2-4 (NIV): "Consider it pure joy, my brothers and sisters, whenever you face trials of many kinds, because you know that the testing of your faith produces perseverance. Let

perseverance finish its work so that you may be mature and complete, not lacking anything."

Restoration and Strength:
- 1 Peter 5:10 (NIV): "And the God of all grace, who called you to his eternal glory in Christ, after you have suffered a little while, will himself restore you and make you strong, firm and steadfast."

Eternal Glory:
- Romans 8:18 (NIV): "I consider that our present sufferings are not worth comparing with the glory that will be revealed in us."

Part 3: Surrender

Trust

THE FIRM BELIEF IN THE RELIABILITY, TRUTH, ABILITY, OR STRENGTH OF SOMEONE OR SOMETHING

Friend, I'm so glad you have made it to this chapter of the book. There is a divine invitation from God for you on the next page: the invitation to surrender. While you have surrendered your life to the Lord when you accepted Him as your Savior, this invitation also calls you to surrender your future plans. I can't pinpoint a date or a specific moment in my life when the Lord invited me to surrender my desire for marriage. It was more like a gradual process, shaped by months, perhaps even years, of pain leading me to listen to the stirring of the Holy Spirit - a stirring that led me face to face with a decision. I was in my early thirties when I felt God called me to sit and talk with Him. So, I met with God and had a conversation that began like this…

"Come, let's talk." He said. I turned off all the noise, sat in the quiet of my living room, and took a breath.
"Ok, God, I'm here."
"I know you want a husband."
"Yes, I want to get married someday…soon."
"What if I don't give you a husband?
"Oh, no," I whispered.
"What if you're single for the rest of your life?" That wasn't the future I had prayed for. It felt as though it would crush me.
"If I don't give you a marriage, what will your response be? Will you still love me?"

    That's not what I wanted to hear, but there was no way I could turn my back on the Lord. My mind could not begin to imagine what life would be like without walking in His presence, knowing comfort and peace and the promise of eternal life. No, I couldn't bear the idea of living apart from the Lord. With a shattered heart, but my spirit knew something deeper - that choosing the Lord will always be the right decision.

    Here's the prompt I feel compelled by the Holy Spirit to present to you: If the Lord were to say no to marriage for your life, what would your response be? Will you still love and serve Him? This might not be the direction you expected the book to take. Still, as you move on to the next pages, I encourage you to open your heart to have this dialogue with the Lord. How will you respond to God if your plans don't unfold as you planned?

I never really learned how to swim. Sure, I took swimming lessons as a kid, but my parents rarely took me swimming. I never dared to go too deep in a pool. If my feet could not touch the bottom, I would move my arms and legs, trying to grab onto something, but panic would immediately tire me. But you know what's funny? The one thing I do remember is how to lay back and float. If I could just stop wrestling with the water and lay back, I would be carried by the water to safety. In the same way, surrendering to the Lord is not about wrestling the unknown or *losing* strength. It's about leaning on *His* strength trusting Him to hold your head up.

"Trust" seems to be a recurring theme for the single woman, doesn't it? People's well-meaning advice about my singleness often ended with this one thing: "Just keep trusting in the Lord." In response, I would nod and say, "Of course I will." Yet inwardly, I couldn't help but wonder, "Umm, do you really think I'm not?"

When I took a moment to look up the definition of trust, what I found was like a breath of fresh air. Let's take a moment to reconsider the meaning of trust, offering us a fresh perspective on this familiar word.

TRUST:
- FIRM BELIEF IN THE RELIABILITY, TRUTH, ABILITY, OR STRENGTH OF SOMEONE OR SOMETHING.

Let's take that definition and change "someone" to "God". Now, read it this way...

Trust
- The firm belief in the reliability *of* God.
- The firm belief in the truth *of* God.
- The firm belief in the ability *of* God.
- The firm belief in the strength *of* God.

Whew! You see, trusting in God is not about *our* strength. It is about *His* unwavering reliability, absolute truth, boundless ability, and immeasurable strength. We place our faith in *His* capabilities, not on our own. It doesn't matter whether your grasp is firm or if you are barely holding on with a pinky; when we declare trust in Him, we are affirming, "I trust in who *you* are, and therefore, my future is well." This is *who* we surrender our lives and desires to - the hands of almighty God.

Process Art

I have been an art teacher for ten years, and one of my favorite art forms to teach is abstract art. When introducing this idea to kids, it may initially seem strange. Naturally, they want their art to look like something they know or have seen before. I invite them to take their blank canvas, grab some paints and brushes, and fearlessly splatter paint and let go. Their instinct is to correct every stroke and clean up the splatter. But when the transition from "I don't like it" to "this is fun!" occurs, it marks a pivotal moment - they forget about trying to make their painting look perfect and enjoy the process. As their teacher, witnessing this transformation fills me with immense joy because, ultimately, it's not so much about the finished product but more about how they got there. This is what we call *process* art.

Surrender is much like process art. It is not linear but rather more abstract. At first, it does not make sense to release our hold on what we want our future to look like, but Christ's work in us through the process is transformative.

Someone once told me they had a dream of a mansion in heaven. In this mansion, there was a long hallway, and on the walls hung paintings. Each artwork represented a different person and the process they went through. These paintings were presented to God, and they would sing to Him. I can't help but think about our lives as paintings adorning the hallways of heaven where God walks through. Every painting worships Him. Can you imagine God passing by your painting, listening to your song, and saying, *"Oh yes, I remember this one. We did this together."*

Friend, what does your painting look like? What does your process sing to God? I turn this question back to you. If God were to respond with a "no" to your desire for marriage, what would your response be?

Let me be a voice in your ear, a voice that has been where you're at, to remind you that it *is* worth it. I stand among many women who have made it to the other side of surrender, cheering you on the sidelines of your race, shouting, *"Jesus is worth it!"*

Jesus, I'm letting go.

Good. I am just getting started.

Draw Near

Imagine your life as a painting adorning the hallways of heaven, singing a song of worship to God. What does your painting represent, and what does your process sing to Him?

The Invitation to Surrender

"If all I have is your presence
then I have everything I need."

  I was able to say the above words to the Lord, and although I did not say these words shouting with joy, I trusted that He would make my joy complete.

  The purpose of this book is to guide you to a place where you can say that even if you don't get this one thing, you are ok because your life rests in His hands. The only way I know where to lead you is into surrender, which led me to this rare and heavenly kind of wholeness and fulfillment. I cannot promise you that you will not have your lows, but this surrender becomes an anchor you can always return to. True wholeness is not a collection of experiences or possessions. In Christ, wholeness is "I have everything even when I don't."

  You have an option today to either live in worry about tomorrow or live in peace no matter what lies ahead. From making it to one more day to welcoming the day, the decision is yours. I am not suggesting you stop praying for a husband. You can still experience wholeness and fulfillment in Christ even as you pray for a husband and navigate dating.

  Do you feel a stirring of the Holy Spirit? I have prayed, firmly believing that God will place this book in the hands of women whose journeys align with divine timing. Surrendering marks the end of one stage in your journey and positions you to begin a new stage with the Lord.

  I pray your life serves as a powerful testimony—a testament to when God truly becomes your portion. May the beauty of your surrender shine as evidence of God's goodness. May it leave a lasting impact and legacy to influence generations to come. Amen.

"Lord, what do you want to say to your daughters?"

"Their thoughts are preoccupied with tomorrow's worries, overwhelmed and overburdened, sometimes even self-critical of their appearance.
Yet, I cherish all that I have created. Oh, how I love what I have made!
I yearn to be their foremost thought.
Dwelling within them.
How fervently I desire their presence!
Every part of their existence is created to draw them nearer to me.
This is the invitation. Bring me your tomorrow's.
Allow me to direct them, for I can guide better than you."

Takeaway Points:

- Trust is not about our strength but believing in God's reliability, truth, ability, and strength. When we declare trust in Him, we affirm His unwavering character and acknowledge His power to shape our future.

- Surrender is like process art—abstract and transformative. Just as children learn to enjoy the creative process without fixating on the end result, we can find joy in surrendering our plans to God, trusting in His guiding hand.
- How would you respond if God answered no to your desire for a husband? Embrace this question and reflect on your willingness to surrender to God's will, knowing He is always worth it.
- As you utter the words, "Jesus, I'm letting go," remember that this is just the beginning. Surrendering is an ongoing process, and as you release control, trust that God is only just getting started in your life.

Conversations with God: Surrender

Before: Find a quiet spot. Pray and ask God to silence your mind.

What if God asked you today to surrender this desire for a husband? How would you respond to Him? This may not be the most exciting dialogue with God; you might even be hesitant to approach it. Yet, I encourage you to have this conversation with God.

> *Picture God sitting beside you, His gaze filled with love as he looks at you.*
> *In His eyes, you sense an unconditional love and devotion that leaves no room for doubt.*
> *With complete trust, you lay your future down.*
> *With eyes on you, He takes hold of your hands, hands that hold the world yet hold yours with utmost care.*
> *He asks you the question you have been avoiding.*
> *"What if a husband and marriage never arrive? Will you still love me?"*
> *Take a breath and look at his eyes - eyes that see everything, eyes that understand all, and overflow with compassion.*
> *Your Heavenly Father's eyes invite you to surrender your future into His hands.*

(Take a breath.)

Write your response in the following lines..

Our ending is the beginning.

Part 4: Whole

Walking In Surrender

"THE FURTHER IN YOU GO, THE LESS YOU TAKE WITH YOU. JESUS, HE BECOMES THE DREAM."
- MICHAEL KOULIANOS

I can't write about wholeness without the name of Jesus. While the world may offer several action steps to wholeness — self-love, self-discovery, self-acceptance, self-improvement, self-gratification - that look like a personal blog on Instagram, true wholeness revolves around Jesus. He becomes the center of our lives - Jesus becomes the dream.

In a culture saturated with self-centered ideas, it is crucial to recognize that for the Christian, wholeness does not have anything to do with self-sufficiency but daily dying to self. Daily surrender might look radical, but as followers of Christ, we're not supposed to blend and look like the world.

My journey to wholeness began when I surrendered my future to the Lord as a single woman. It was a transformative experience, a rare kind of wholeness that I continue to live in as a married woman. My marital status has nothing to do with my wholeness - my husband does not make me whole; Jesus does. I've had my low moments, and you may find yourself in similar situations along your journey. But the beauty lies in knowing that you don't have to stay in that place of despair. You might get deviated here and there, but when Jesus is your home base, you can always come home to Him.

You will find spiritual encouragement and practical steps toward stewarding wholeness as you read the following pages. Still, ultimately, it's essential to recognize that complete wholeness is not an arrival here on earth. We will never get "there". We become whole when we become like Him, and that will happen when we get to heaven. Here on earth, we can have a rare kind of wholeness - peace, joy, and fulfillment through Christ Jesus beyond any circumstance.

In the following pages, I want to share three key points that helped me walk in this life of surrender.

1. Make Jesus the Dream

Seated at the front row of a youth conference in McAllen, TX, I was in the company of over 2,000 young people who gathered to worship God. At 28 years old, I experienced beautiful moments in His presence, but while worshiping at this conference, this moment with God was different. I was on my knees, trying to sing through the tears, when I bowed my head low close to the floor and felt enveloped by God's presence like a blanket wrapped around me. At that moment, a whisper escaped my lips, "God, You can take me." The words were not normal. It was as if it came from someone who did not belong on earth. Yet, in that completeness within His presence, I experienced a glimpse of heaven, and I desired to be *home*. No longer a wanderer, His presence was *home*. In the beauty and holiness of His presence, it was so easy, so natural, to let go of earthly dreams and wants. With just one glimpse of heaven, I could easily leave everything behind because *He* was the prize - the dream.

The more we live in His presence, in this abandonment of our desires, the more we find ourselves embracing Jesus - the ultimate dream and fulfillment of our lives. He is the real treasure.

> "THE FURTHER IN YOU GO, THE LESS YOU TAKE WITH YOU.
> JESUS, HE BECOMES THE DREAM."
> – MICHAEL KOULIANOS

I'm not anyone special. I'm just your average girl, born and raised in the RGV. This depth with God, the revelation I receive from Him - it's not only for me. This nearness I have with the Father is not only reserved for me. He has something reserved uniquely for you, too. All I did was continue to press in again and again. Hunger does that to you. If He's doing it for me, He's got something special lined up for you too.

I'm reminded of Paul's words in Philippians 3, the longing of knowing Christ and participating in His suffering.

7 I once thought these things were valuable, but now I consider them worthless because of what Christ has done.

8 Yes, everything else is worthless when compared with the infinite value of knowing Christ Jesus my Lord. For his sake I have discarded everything else, counting it all as garbage, so that I could gain Christ

10 I want to know Christ and experience the mighty power that raised him from the dead. I want to suffer with him, sharing in his death,

The infinite value of knowing Christ…friend, do we know this? Do we value our relationship with Christ more important than anything else? What a convicting challenge for us today! Evaluating our priorities and recognizing the incomparable value of a relationship with Christ is a challenge. This love for the Lord that Paul had is radical. It may require changes in our daily schedule, life goals, or lifestyle.

Our love for the Lord compels us to let go of everything else, to empty ourselves so we can personally know Christ. It's not merely about knowing *about* Christ but about intimately knowing Him.

This surrender is not seasonal. This is ongoing while we are here on earth. It is until we get to heaven when we will become fully like him.

2. BEAUTY IN SURRENDER

Let me remind you of how profoundly beautiful and holy sacrifice is. How meaningful it is to deny ourselves and take up our cross to follow Jesus, even when it goes against the grain of our culture. Sacrifice - selfless, sacred, and to some, even radical - is the kind of life the Lord calls his people to strive for, to be holy as He is holy (1 Peter 1:15-16).

In a world consumed by "self," it's easy for the true essence of sacrifice to get lost. While all these "self" pursuits contribute to nurturing our well-being, I pray we open our hearts to the conviction of the Holy Spirit so our "well" is found in Him, the creator of our being.

As we dive more into this sacrificial living, there are treasures to uncover as we walk in surrender.

1. In surrendering our lives, we get the profound privilege of being imitators of Christ's sacrificial love by offering ourselves as living sacrifices and reflecting His love and grace to the world. You literally get to be a walking, living sacrifice - daily surrendering your will to God's perfect purposes. This is your act of worship, allowing Him to use your singleness and every aspect of your life for His glory. Ephesians 5:1-2
2. Sacrifice is a tangible expression of love for God. It's not just about giving something up; it's a way to show our deep love for God in tangible ways. 1 John 3:16
3. Sacrifice has a transformative effect on our character and soul. God takes our messes and molds us into something beautiful. A spiritual makeover with results always being stunning! Romans 12:1-2
4. Sacrifice shifts one's focus from temporal to eternal values. Helps us to see beyond the here and now, investing in what truly after - the kingdom of God. Matthew 6:19-21

5. Sacrifice leaves a lasting impact and legacy. They are like planting seeds of faithfulness and blessing for generations to come. Proverbs 13:22

3. SPIRIT OF CONTENTMENT

In my 20s, it seemed like everyone was curious about my dating life. Questions about boyfriends and relationships were pretty common. My answer typically sounded something like I was trusting in God's timing: "As long as I'm doing God's will, He will make it happen." It felt like a safe and reassuring answer, rooted in the belief that as long as I was doing all the right things, living well, and waiting well, it would inevitably lead to my husband showing up at the right time. While there's some truth to this, something changed in my perspective.

I realized that this idea I believed in, 'Waiting well equals getting what I want,' was not aligned with the gospel. Waiting well does not guarantee a husband. God didn't promise us equal outcomes, *but* He did promise us His presence.

In my early 30s, after I surrendered my future to the Lord, the more I walked in surrender and deepened my relationship with Him, the more *content* I became - genuinely happy with what I had and where I was in life. This kind of contentment goes against modern culture. There's this constant push around us to have more, do more, be more. But let me tell you a little secret: contentment is not an automatic response. It doesn't magically happen overnight. Especially when you're facing seasons of lack or uncertainty, finding contentment requires growth and maturity in your faith and gets easier through experience. It's a journey, friend.

In Philippians 4:11-13, Paul had some pretty wise words to say about contentment, he even shared his secret of being content.

*"I am not saying this because I am in need,
for I have learned to be content whatever the circumstances.
I know what it is to be in need, and I know what it is to have plenty.
I have learned the secret of being content in any and every situation, whether well fed or hungry, whether living in plenty or in want.
I can do all this through him who gives me strength."*
Philippians 4:11-13

Paul knew what it was like to have plenty and be in need. He'd been through it all. This indicates a broad range of life experiences contributing to his understanding of contentment. Do you want to know Paul's secret to contentment? His secret is in Jesus - the strength he receives from Christ. It is not a result of his own efforts or willpower but is made possible through the strength that comes from his union with Christ—the power of his relationship with Jesus.

I used to think that contentment meant settling for less, *Well, I guess this is all I'll ever have, so I might as well be happy with what I've got.* It felt like a poverty mindset, with a whole bunch of negativity attached. *You're content because you don't have ambition. You're not fighting hard. You're not praying hard.* No, friend. It's not about pretending everything is perfect or ignoring our dreams and desires. You can live in contentment and have ambition, have joy in the Lord, and still desire for more.

But here's the key: it's about where those desires come from. When your dreams are rooted in your trust and faith in God, they do not grow from a place of lack. They grow from healthy soil.

So, let's flip the script on contentment. Your prayer for a husband doesn't have to come from a place of feeling lonely or lacking. It can come from a place of living life to the fullest, from a heart that's overflowing with joy and gratitude.

Just A Few Practical Steps

Spiritual and practicality go hand in hand. I want to share some practical steps to cultivate and walk in this rare kind of wholeness in Christ Jesus.

1. Gratitude: It's difficult to be discontent when you are consistently practicing and expressing gratitude. When we're not so focused on what we lack or what's going wrong, we're filled with this deep sense of appreciation for the abundance of blessings all around us. Begin a daily gratitude journal, record a daily voice memo to practice saying it out loud, and begin a gratitude message thread with friends to keep yourselves accountable for practicing gratitude. However you choose to do it, do it!

2. Environment: Create an environment through a supportive community. Be intentional about friendships and nurture them. If you do not have a group of friends, take the risk

and ask if you can join one or create your own. When I needed friendships, I started reaching out to young women and planning get-togethers at my house. You might be the one to bring people together. You also have the help of the Holy Spirit to guide you in seeing who needs your friendship.

3. Mental and Physical Health: Seek professional counseling and prioritize your health. Our responsibility is to take care of our well-being and steward our bodies. This, too, is an expression of love for God. God deeply cares about how we take care of our bodies so much that he will give us a new one when we get to heaven.

4. Spiritual Growth: You know this one, and you are doing this so well. Spiritual growth is character growth. Keep having those intimate conversations with your heavenly father. Keep growing in the fruits of the spirit - the evidence of the Holy Spirit in you. I also encourage you to fast. Fasting is a weapon for breakthrough and depth in Christ.

Takeaway Points:

- By surrendering earthly dreams and wants, we can find fulfillment in embracing Jesus as our ultimate dream and treasure.
- The passage from Philippians underscores the incomparable value of knowing Christ and experiencing

the power of His resurrection. This calls us to reflect on our relationship with Christ and our desire to know Him more intimately.

- The chapter emphasizes the beauty and holiness of sacrifice, challenging and convicting us to reevaluate our priorities and embrace sacrificial living in obedience to God's call to holiness.
- True contentment isn't automatic; it's a journey that requires growth and maturity in our faith. Even amidst seasons of lack or uncertainty, we can cultivate contentment by deepening our relationship with God and trusting in His provision.
- Contentment isn't about settling for less or ignoring our desires. It's about finding joy and satisfaction in our present circumstances while pursuing our dreams with ambition. When our desires are rooted in trust and faith in God, they come from a place of abundance rather than lack.

Draw Near

Consider the ongoing nature of surrender in the Christian life, as mentioned in the passage. How can you cultivate a mindset of continual surrender in your relationship with God? What steps can you take to ensure that your love for the Lord remains steadfast and unwavering?

_____
_____
_____
_____
_____
_____
_____
_____
_____
_____
_____
_____
_____
_____
_____
_____
_____

Journal about any fears or hesitations you may have regarding sacrifice and surrender. What obstacles or challenges do you face in fully embracing these concepts in your life?

What are some other ways you can cultivate a spirit of contentment? What practices will you change, and what will you begin applying?

_____
_____
_____
_____
_____
_____
_____
_____
_____
_____
_____
_____
_____
_____
_____
_____
_____
_____
_____
_____

Epilogue

The Recipe

"Ahni, what was the recipe?" my counselor, Kathy, asked.

"The recipe?" I repeated, unsure.

"Yes. The steps you took to come out of depression then, you can use those same steps now in this season." I had never heard it that way. I sat in Kathy's counseling room and noticed a flood of memories of how the Lord moved in my past. I accepted the tissue Kathy offered and took a deep breath.

"So, what was the recipe?" she prompted again, gentle yet probing.

"*Jesus*," I answered quietly, uttering his name, my voice quivering and my eyes welling up with tears—the name of Jesus… the name of *Jesus*. Closing my eyes, I noticed memories of how the Lord moved in my past, and I remembered several steps I had taken to get out of those dark valleys.

I do have a recipe for those dark valleys, and so do you. You and I have been through storms, crying out for help many times. And on some of those occasions, the Lord did not stop the storm, but he walked them alongside you, ever-present by your side. What were some of the tools that helped you navigate through? Was it fasting, calling a trusted friend as a prayer partner, meeting for coffee with a mentor, scheduling a session with your counselor, or waking up early to meet with God? What carried you through the storm? That, my friend, is your recipe, and you will use it again and again for those moments or seasons that feel like dips. Remember, it's just a dip, not a tomb.

In the journey of singleness, feelings of loneliness, being unchosen, and memories of shame may resurface at times, but you now have a recipe for navigating those seasons. This recipe not only sustains you but also serves as a powerful testimony for others. Another year single, another holiday single, another birthday single, and yet, blessed are you.

> **OUR JOURNEY HERE ON EARTH IS A MYSTERY SURROUNDED BY THE PROMISE OF HIS PRESENCE.**
> ///////////////////

(Check out "Beyond the Pages" on page 154 for a bonus exercise to create your recipe.)

Fireworks

In 2015, my little sister Mimi and I spent a few weeks in California. We decided to stop at Disneyland just for fun. Two twenty-year-olds laughing like little kids on the Little Mermaid ride remains a memory I will always cherish. As the sun set, everyone gathered by the Ferris wheel with the giant Mickey Mouse face. Cinematic music began playing, and color lit up the sky: fireworks! "Ohs" and "ahs" were heard through the crowd while children sat on their dad's shoulders, pointing to the sky. I couldn't help but notice a sweet moment between a couple, their arms wrapped around each other. Their eyes met, and they kissed. It was sweet. It was also lonely.

    I remembered other moments when fireworks flooded the sky: Fourth of July celebrations, theme park visits, and evenings at the beach. In every memory, I was surrounded by family or friends, and I still felt lonely. This time, at 28 years of age, standing in front of the giant Mickey Mouse face, that familiar ache returned. In a hushed whisper, I confessed to God, "*God, I want a firework moment.*"

In 2021, on a Wednesday night in April, I received a notification from a dating app that a family friend, Shirley, insisted I try. My pride kept me from joining a dating app. I wanted to have a romantic story of how I met my husband, something straight out of a rom-com movie: perhaps we bumped into each other at a coffee shop, or maybe a moment of clumsiness where I spilled coffee on a handsome stranger. But at 34, that never happened.

So, while visiting Shirley, she sat me in her living room and convinced me to try online dating. "When you are in high school, high school students are your pool of potential matches. In college, college students are your pool of potential matches. Today, your pool is church and work, but that pool offers limited options. You've got to open up your pool, and that is through online dating." That sounded like a good reason. So, I jumped on a Christian dating app. After several weeks on the dating app, I received a message from *Matt Hancock*. That same night, I replied to Matt (and stalked him a little on Facebook and Instagram, not gonna' lie). We exchanged numbers on the third day and had our first phone call on the fifth day. We talked about our lives, families, and dreams. I loved his voice (mhmm!) and loved hearing a personal God in his testimony. We ended the call, and I said to the Lord, "Jesus, I want that one."

We continued getting to know each other, and we both knew very early on that this was something special. It was so easy talking to Matt, so natural. As our relationship continued to grow, we both felt peace.

After two and a half months of talking, I flew to Louisiana to meet Matt in person. My plane landed in Monroe on a Friday evening in July, and giiiirrrrl...I almost didn't get off that plane! *OMG, what am I doing?!* I was the last person to get off the plane, and I found a restroom to hide for a minute and take deep breaths. *Will he like me? Will he be disappointed? Oh, man, maybe I used too many filters on my photos!*

Well, I wasn't in South Texas anymore. No more chamoyadas and elotes en vaso. I was in Louisiana, the land of crawfish and jambalaya, about to meet face-to-face with a man from a dating app. I walked out of the restroom, looked past security, and saw Matt standing looking back at me. That weekend, I met his parents and kids, took a tour of his workplace, and drove around in his truck. As we drove, I looked out the window at his small town, imagining what life would be like if I were to make this place my home, picturing these very roads that could one day take me to *our* home. After that weekend visit, I knew I wanted to wake up to his face every morning, fall asleep beside him every night, and love him for the rest of my life.

Matt was in the valley for a weekend in October, and we decided to spend our Saturday evening at South Padre Island. We were both sitting quietly on a restaurant porch facing the ocean, taking in the moment when I felt a sweet presence of heaven, so strong yet so peaceful, cover us. I heard the words, "This is right," affirming that God was pleased with us in our journey together. I grabbed Matt's arm, looked at him, and said, "Matt, I am really happy."

After our dinner, the sun began to set, and we walked by the water. We walked away from the crowds until we were alone. Matt started talking about the Lord, answering prayers, and redeeming His life. I wish I could remember the rest of what he said, but it is all a blur because Matt took a ring out of his pocket, got on one knee, and asked me to be his wife.

As we returned to the restaurant, I repeatedly looked at my left hand, almost in disbelief, as if needing reassurance that what I felt was real—I was engaged. It was nighttime, and music began playing when suddenly lights illuminated the sky: fireworks! God gave me a firework moment.

On December 29th, 2021, Matt and I exchanged vows and started a new journey as husband and wife.

Friend, this is my testimony, a glimpse of what God has done in my life. I don't know what He has in store for you. I can't give you a step-by-step solution to finding a husband because I don't always understand God's ways. But I can offer a testimony about the goodness and faithfulness of the Father and of this rare kind of wholeness and fulfillment that He gives to his beloved daughters. Looking back, I can now see purpose in every moment of feeling overlooked, disappointed, left out, and let down. E-v-e-r-y-t-h-i-n-g has a purpose. Every experience, every emotion - each has played a vital role in shaping my journey. And I can't help but think about John 9:3, where Jesus explains why a man was born blind and healed him, saying, "But this happened so that the works of God might be displayed in him." I pray that my life becomes a painting that glorifies Him. Just as my life serves as a testament to His greatness, so does yours.

Do not stop praying for a husband. Continue to lift your prayer, but now, you don't have to pray out of a place of lack. You pray out of a place of trust - knowing that God has your surrendered life in His hands. Your plans are released to the hands of a faithful and trustworthy God. And, oh, how He loves you.

To end this book, I want to end with a personalized prayer over you…

Psalm 139

O Lord, you have examined her heart
    and know everything about her.
You know when she sits down or stands up.
    You know her thoughts even when she is far away.

You see her when she travels
    and when she rests at home.
    You know everything she does.

You know what she is going to say
    even before she says it, Lord.

You go before her and follow her.
    You place your hand of blessing on her head.

Such knowledge is too wonderful for her,
    too great for her to understand!

She can never escape from your Spirit!
    She can never get away from your presence!

If she goes up to heaven, you are there;
    if she goes down to the grave, you are there.

If she rides the wings of the morning,
    if she dwells by the farthest oceans,

even there your hand will guide her,
>   and your strength will support her.

She could ask the darkness to hide her
>   and the light around her to become night—

>   but even in darkness she cannot hide from you.
>   To you the night shines as bright as day.
>   Darkness and light are the same to you.

You made all the delicate, inner parts of her body
>   and knit her together in her mother's womb.

Thank you for making her so wonderfully complex!
>   Your workmanship is marvelous—how well I know it.

You watched her as she was being formed in utter seclusion,
>   as she was woven together in the dark of the womb.

You saw her before she was born.
>   Every day of her life was recorded in your book.
>   Every moment was laid out
>   before a single day had passed.

How precious are your thoughts about her, O God.
>   They cannot be numbered!

She can't even count them;
>   they outnumber the grains of sand!

And when she wakes up,
 you are still with her!

Amen.

(I asked my husband to write to you. I thought it would be powerful for you to hear from a man cheering you on.)

From Matt

I have the honor and privilege of knowing Ahni in ways no one else ever will…and that is because I am the man who is blessed to be her husband. She and I have spent months and months over the past two years in deep conversations about this book and its message, so I know her heart for you. I know her compassion for you. I've seen the tears in her eyes, and I've heard her voice break when she has described the pain and struggles she bravely faced as a single woman. I hope *you* have sensed how much she cares for you, but even more importantly, I hope you have sensed God's great love for you.

It is an honor for me to write to you and share a little bit from behind the curtain…or better yet, from the beautiful shores that await on the other side of what can, at times, appear to be an impossible storm. A few things I'd like to ask you to consider: One, no two stories are alike, but the Jesus who commanded the winds and waves is the same Jesus who sees you…hears you…

and has your best at heart. It's one thing to say that, and it's one thing to say you believe it…but truly believing it opens your eyes and your heart to wonders and blessings beyond compare. Do you believe these things in the depths of your soul? Ahni did when she was in your position, and she continues to. One of the most humbling experiences of my life was reading the journal Ahni wrote that contained the prayers she prayed for her future husband (notice the belief and faith). She had never met, seen, or even heard of me, and yet she prayed for me because she genuinely believed I existed somewhere in the world. She also had no way of knowing that during that very specific season in time, when she was going to the Father on *my* behalf, my life and previous marriage were being torn apart. Her faith and belief that I existed prompted her to love me before we ever met…and I believe it contributed to my survival of the most painful season of my life.

    Two, what appears to be the silence of God can be very painful; it seems as if we don't matter to Him, but I have learned that not only does He care for us beyond what we can fathom, He also grieves with us over the pains of life in a broken world. Sometimes, the best thing our closest friend can do is to quietly listen, to sit *with* us in the pain. Look for His presence. Draw near to Him with an expectant heart because His Word says He is near to the brokenhearted (Psalms 34:18). His Word also promises that if we draw near to Him, He will draw near to us (James 4:8). And then remain in Him (John 15:5) so that your life will bear the fruit that draws others to Him.

    Ahni did that. Ahni *does* that. I am always proud to say that as much as she loves me, she loves Jesus *more*. She loves Jesus first, and I wouldn't have it any other way. Ahni is the epitome of a Proverbs 31 woman…but she sought to be that long before she became a wife. Men who love the Lord love peace and honor, faithfulness, and a true partner, and we seek to love our wives and live our lives in this way because it is pleasing to God.

Finally, I would urge you to take responsibility for every aspect of your life. All your feelings, all your emotions…your actions, reactions, thoughts, and beliefs are your responsibility. I don't make Ahni happy. Ahni is happy because she has chosen to be. We don't depend on each other for our happiness or joy or contentment, and yet you won't find two people who are happier, more joyful, or more content. We were both doing this before we met, and I was so thankful that God brought me a woman who understood this.

In November 2020, I told God everything I wanted in marriage, and the moment I began praying, He set the wheels in motion (Daniel 9:23). Six months later, He had cleared the way to bring Ahni to me and three years later, He has answered every prayer with 100% accuracy. Sometimes, the clearing of the road is painful…having your heart refined in the fires of suffering is excruciating at times, but let your faith in Him carry you. It took me 20 years to make it to my soulmate. It hurt. At times, I felt I couldn't go on. There were days in which it seemed that dying would be easier, but I'm so glad that I held to the promises of Mathew 28:20, "…and surely I am with you always, to the very end of the age."

I don't know what the pages of your story will contain. I don't know what the Lord has in store for you. You see, God doesn't promise us equity in this life…even for us as believers. Sometimes, we look around at what others have, and we can feel like *we* deserve those same things…maybe sometimes we wrongly believe we deserve those things more than those who *do* have them (Ouch!), but God doesn't promise us equity. He has, however, promised to never leave us or forsake us. In fact, He has promised to be with us always…and He has promised us a home…with Him.

Friend, your identity will never be found in prosperity, or a big home, in children, or in a husband. Your identity is in Jesus! If you've been searching for your identity, I've just given you the map to that treasure. Jesus is your treasure. He is your everything, and if you rest in Him and trust Him with your prayers, you will be amazed of what becomes of your life! And guess what? He will surprise you!

I've become convinced that this is God's beautiful equation. It's not easy, but it is beautiful in its simplicity. If you are reading this, I believe you are rare and beautiful, but don't pursue being a "rare woman" for the sake of getting what you want. Pursue it because that way of living honors your blessed Savior! And should God bless you with a husband, that will be what my people call "lagniappe" (a little something extra). Pursue holiness above all, and God will use you and your life in ways you can scarcely imagine. *That* is your calling above all else, dearest sister. Take joy in that. Keep leaning on His everlasting arms. If you do that, and if you trust and believe the promises from His Word, you will walk daily in something most people will never experience…the joy of the Lord…Jesus will be more than enough…and *your* song through endless ages will be: "Jesus led me all the way!"

- Matt Hancock

Group Discussion Starters

Introduction

Rare

1. Have you ever experienced a situation similar to what the author describes in the doctor's office? How did it make you feel, and how did you respond?

2. How do societal norms and expectations regarding relationships and sexuality impact single Christian women today? Have you ever felt pressured to conform to these norms?

3. Reflecting on the checklist provided, how do you relate to the concept of being "rare" as a single Christian woman? Do you resonate with any of the listed qualities or experiences?

4. How can we, as single Christian women, support and encourage one another in embracing our uniqueness and living counterculturally according to Christian principles?

5. In what ways can we shine the light of Christ in a world that often devalues singleness and purity? How can we uphold a standard of purity and faith while navigating societal pressures?

6. What practical steps can we take to cultivate a deeper longing for God's presence above all other desires and to embrace the rare kind of living described in the book?

Part 1: Identity

He Prepares A Place

1. Share a time when you struggled with unanswered "why" questions in your relationship with God. How did you navigate those feelings of uncertainty or doubt?

2. Reflect on God's message as shared in the chapter. How does it challenge or affirm your understanding of God's love and presence in your life?

3. Reflect on the invitation to take God's hand again and embrace the journey of reconnecting with Him. What does this invitation mean to you personally, and how do you plan to respond to it?

Testify

1. Have you ever felt hesitant to share a struggle because of fear of being shamed or judged by others?

2. In what ways can we create environments in our churches or communities where people feel safe to share their struggles without fear of judgment or shame?

3. How does God's kindness and patience towards us inspire us to extend the same to others who may be struggling?

4. What steps can we take individually and collectively to embrace our weaknesses and vulnerabilities as opportunities for God's grace and redemption in our lives?

Part 2: Lament

He Sits In The Dark With Us

1. Have you ever experienced a moment where you felt like God's plan for your life was crumbling before your eyes? How did you cope with that situation?

2. In moments of darkness and despair, have you ever felt the tangible presence of God comforting you, even when you couldn't see or hear Him?

3. Can you relate to the experience of feeling hurt or betrayed by God, even though deep down, you know He loves you? How did you reconcile those conflicting emotions?

4. How do you balance expressing your honest emotions with maintaining trust and faith in God's plan for your life?

5. Have you ever found yourself repeating prayers or lines that sound cliche, but don't truly reflect your genuine feelings? How do you ensure your communication with God remains authentic?

6. What role do you think lamentation plays in our spiritual journey? How can embracing our pain and expressing it to God lead to deeper intimacy with Him?

7. How can we learn from the psalmists' example of moving from lament to expressions of trust and hope in God? What practical steps can we take to cultivate a similar attitude in our own lives?

Part 3: Surrender

Trust:

1. Reflect on a time in your life when you had to surrender a desire or plan to God. What was your initial response, and how did you eventually come to surrender?

2. Consider the scenario presented in the chapter: If God were to say no to a specific desire or plan in your life, how would you respond? How does your trust in God influence your response to His plans?

3. How can surrendering to God's will lead to wholeness and fulfillment, even in the midst of waiting or uncertainty? Have you experienced this in your own life?

4. Reflect on the imagery of your life as a painting hanging on the walls of heaven. What do you envision your painting singing to God? How does this perspective impact your understanding of surrender?

Part 4: Whole

Jesus Is The Dream

1. Share a moment from your own life when you felt a profound encounter with God's presence. How did this experience impact your faith journey?

2. Discuss the concept of embracing Jesus as the ultimate dream and treasure of our lives. How does this perspective challenge common beliefs of success and fulfillment?

3. Consider the idea of surrendering to God as an ongoing process rather than a one-time event. What are some practical steps we can take to continually surrender to God's will and trust in His plan for our lives?

4. How did you initially view the concept of waiting well, especially in relation to finding a spouse? Did you share the belief that doing all the right things would inevitably lead to finding a spouse?

5. Have you ever struggled with the idea that contentment means settling for less? How does the biblical perspective on contentment differ from this mindset?

6. Consider the notion that contentment can coexist with ambition and a desire for more. How can we cultivate a healthy balance between contentment in the present and aspirations for the future?

Beyond the Pages

Next Steps

How do you see yourself in the future? Envision a time when you have fully embraced healing and freedom from the shame associated with this part of your life. Describe what your life looks like and how you feel in the future.

Who can you reach out to for help? What will keep you from reaching out for help? Consider reaching out to a trusted Christian friend, mentor, or pastor for support and accountability as you navigate through this process of bringing your struggle into God's light.

_____

_____

_____

_____

_____

_____

_____

_____

_____

_____

_____

_____

_____

_____

_____

_____

_____

_____

_____

_____

What action steps are your next steps? What resources or support systems are available to help you navigate through this struggle? This could include therapy, trusted friends or mentors, books, or online resources.

Fasting is such a powerful weapon for the Christian. It's not only meant for the beginning of the year; fasting is a pathway to your breakthrough. If you're unfamiliar with fasting, I encourage you to dive into resources like books or sermons. Pray and ask God to show you how He wants you to incorporate fasting into your life.

Tracing God's Presence

    In this exercise, you will create a timeline of your life, highlighting those pivotal moments and seasons that have shaped who you are today. Think of these experiences as your very own Ebenezer stones—reminders of God's goodness and faithfulness in your journey. What were once painful or unwanted memories now stand as a testimony to His grace and provision. Take some time to reflect on how God showed up during those times and what blessings emerged as a result. You'll have a chance to draw it all out on the next page.

    This visual timeline will serve as a powerful declaration of God's intervention in your life. It's a tangible reminder that, no matter what, He has always been present, faithfully guiding and shaping your story.

    This reflection would also be a great idea to do with friends. Gather your friends and get some posters, collage paper, and pretty markers. Together, create a timeline of significant events in your lives. Reflect on how God has been present, intervened, and taught you valuable lessons along the way. (See next page.)

Tracing God's Presence

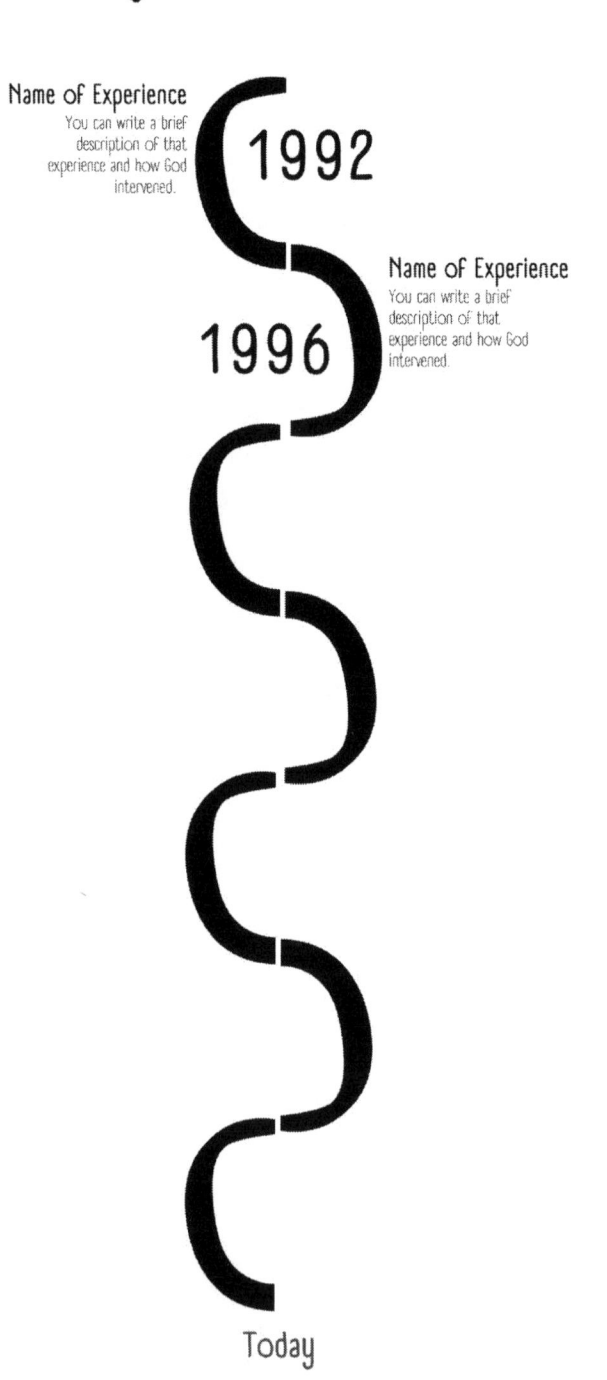

Name of Experience
You can write a brief description of that experience and how God intervened.

1992

1996

Name of Experience
You can write a brief description of that experience and how God intervened.

Today

The Recipe

    I've put together this worksheet to help you create your very own recipe – one that you can turn to whenever life throws you a curveball. Reflect on the steps you've taken to navigate through difficult seasons in your life.

    Think back on the strategies you've used to weather those storms—whether it's fasting, seeking counsel, or connecting with trusted friends. These are the ingredients that have helped you build resilience and navigate through the dips in your journey of singleness. Whatever it is, jot it down and make it your own recipe for resilience.

    Once you've found a recipe for healing that works for you, don't hesitate to share it with others who may be going through similar struggles. Your experiences and insights could be just what someone else needs to find their way through the storm. (See next page.)

Recipe for...

"_____"

Ingredients

_____
_____
_____
_____
_____
_____
_____
_____
_____

Cooking Time:
Healing takes time and patience. Be gentle with yourself and continue to trust in God's reliability, truth, ability, and strength. ♡

Notes

References

Smithberger, Andrea. "Women watch Porn Too." Regeneration Website, https://www.regenerationministries.org/women-watch-porn/#

Index

Rare, Oxford Learner's Dictionaries, https://www.oxfordlearnersdictionaries.com/us/definition/english/rare, Accessed December 2023

Counterculture, Vocabulary.Com, https://www.vocabulary.com/dictionary/counterculture#:~:text=A group of people who,about raising children, for example. Accessed February 2024

Trust, Oxford Learner's Dictionaries, https://www.oxfordlearnersdictionaries.com/us/definition/english/trust_1?q=trust, Accessed November 2023

Acknowledgments

To my incredible girlfriends - Johanna, Mariel, Areli, Mitzy, Marina, Itzy, Tanya, Deseray, Jan, Erica, and Adri - your ladies have played a big role in this book. Gathering at my home, we shared countless moments of laughter, tears, and heartfelt conversations with Jesus at the center. Your transparency and friendship have been a constant source of inspiration and encouragement throughout this journey.

Viviane - I wish more young women had the opportunity to be seen and mentored by a strong, wise, and spirit-led woman like you. Thank you for always making time to see me and for your powerful words in this book.

Matt - my love and my gift - your unwavering belief in me and this book has been my rock. Thank you for talking to God and asking Him to help me when I felt stuck. You have been my biggest supporter, cheerleader, and the greatest blessing in my life.

About the Author

Ahni Hancock, a wife, believer, and teacher, resides in North Louisiana with her husband, Matt. Born and raised in South Texas, Ahni's life took a transformative turn when she met Matt on a Christian dating app, prompting her to relocate and make a new home in North Louisiana. In South Texas, she initiated and led Crowns, a women's ministry that hosted empowering conferences for young women. With a significant portion of her life spent as a single woman, Ahni brings invaluable lessons from the waiting to her readers, having met Matt at the age of 34. What sets Ahni apart is her remarkable hospitality—her home in South Texas served as a haven for friends, hosting countless girls' nights filled with laughter, tears, and deep conversations centered around Jesus. In her debut book, "Another Year Single," Ahni invites readers to experience the warmth and authenticity of her living room conversations, making them feel like cherished friends. Described by many as calm, sweet, and radiating with love for the Lord, Ahni's writing is sure to inspire and uplift readers on their own journeys of faith and waiting.

Made in the USA
Columbia, SC
23 May 2024